Xenoph
Th

Vladimir Zhelvis

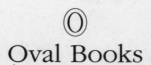

Oval Books

Published by Oval Books
335 Kennington Road
London SE11 4QE
United Kingdom

Telephone: +44 (0)20 7582 7123
Fax: +44 (0)20 7582 1022
E-mail: info@ovalbooks.com
Web site: www.ovalbooks.com

First printed 2001

Editor – Catriona Tulloch Scott
Series Editor – Anne Tauté

Cover designer – Jim Wire, Quantum
Printer – Cox & Wyman Ltd
Producer – Oval Projects Ltd

Xenophobe's® is a Registered Trademark.

Cover: for their matryoshka, thanks are given to
The Russia House, specialists in travel, visa and
accommodation for Russia and the Republics:

The Russia House, 55 Southwark Street
London SE1 1RU
Tel: +44 (0)20 7450 3262
E-mail: russiahouse@btinternet.com

ISBN: 1-902825-41-1

Contents

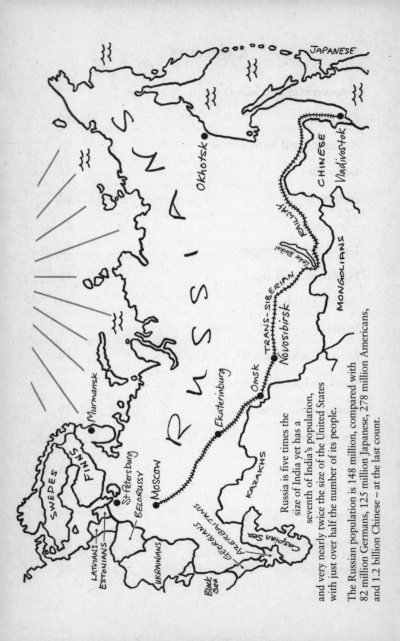

Russia is five times the size of India yet has a seventh of India's population, and very nearly twice the size of the United States with just over half the number of its people.

The Russian population is 148 million, compared with 82 million Germans, 125 million Japanese, 278 million Americans, and 1.2 billion Chinese – at the last count.

Nationalism and Identity

Forewarned

"You're squalid and you're abundant, you're mighty and you're powerless, Mother Russia!" said Nekrasov, the 19th-century Russian poet. Every nation's character is full of contradictory and mutually excluding traits, but Russia's takes a lot of beating. The average Russian is a melancholic who hopes for the best while busily preparing for the worst. Often these preparations are well founded. "Just my luck!" a Russian will exclaim ruefully as another misfortune befalls him. Muttering curses, he will collect the scattered remnants of his belongings and start life anew.

This might suggest that Russians are not patriots. They are, but their patriotism is of a particular kind. What is 'mine' or 'ours' is private and personal, associated with home and native land, while government at any level is 'them', the eternal opponent, who should be feared and avoided. The Government by definition cannot be any good. Nor does anyone expect it to be. As popular wisdom has it: 'Thank God, the store of fools in Russia will last for another hundred years.' It's a healthy pessimism that often helps Russians to avoid disaster.

At the same time, while there's life there's hope. There have been many rainy days, but each time they were followed by sunshine. Weren't they? One has to admit that at present there are rather more rainy days than sunny ones. Russia is at the crossroads, and the best minds of the nation are scratching their heads, uncertain as to which direction she may take.

As is often said: 'Over there across the sea it might be a lot of fun, but it's somebody else's fun. Here at home we might have grief, but it's all ours'.

This is the Russians, strange and naïve, enigmatic and simplistic. Sometimes one wonders how they can really survive in such a combination of sorrow and joy.

How Russians See Themselves

Ask Russians how they see themselves and their answer will reflect the mood they are in. And since for 23 hours a day they feel blue, the answer will probably be that they are the unluckiest and unhappiest nation possible, that things were much better in Communist times, that they were even better under the Czars, and absolutely marvellous in the days of the Vikings. After this, they will fall upon your chest and wash it with sweet tears.

In a happier mood, they will probably say that they are the kindest, most hospitable and friendliest nation the world has ever seen, which is much closer to the truth.

So, one moment you will be told that nobody cares for Russia, that it is the dumbest and most backward backyard of the civilized world; and the next moment the same people will tell you that without Russia the world will go to pieces. "My Russia is so special!" every Russian will tell you in a low voice trembling with emotion. Certainly it's special. Very special. In fact, half this specialness would be quite enough.

How They Think Others See Them

Well, naturally, the whole world knows that Russia is 'The Third Rome', the Saviour of long-suffering Mankind, in short, a Messiah. The Russian coat-of-arms, the double-headed eagle, has its heads turned in opposite directions, one to the West, the other to the East, and for good reason. For Russia is destined to mediate between the two, being neither a Western nor an Oriental country. Sitting between two stools is a very convenient position for a judge. The fact that East is East and West is West, and neither seems to be an ardent disciple of Russia, does not trouble her in the least. Her time will come.

Meanwhile Russians glumly suspect that Westerners

see them as long-bearded muzhiks in big fur caps driving sledges harnessed by troikas of polar bears down the frozen Volga. There might even be a couple of nuclear rockets in those sledges, as well as a bottle of vodka. (Between ourselves, there are two bottles, but that's really neither here nor there.)

It takes time for foreigners to realize that the word 'Russians' implies only part of the population of the Russian Federation. Foreigners often speak about the population of Russia as 'Russians' which offends the numberless non-Russians – Ukranians, Byelorussians, Bashkirs, Kalmyks, Karelians – hundreds of peoples, many of whom live in national autonomous republics with local governments of their own.

The misunderstanding is aggravated by the necessity to differentiate between an ethnic Russian and a Russian citizen of a different nationality but for whom Russia is his native land. New Russian postage stamps have 'Rossija' on them instead of 'Russia'. If the name stays, then you will be called Russian if you are an ethnic Russian. If you are one of the hundreds of national minorities, you will be called a Rossijanin, a citizen of Rossija. This is sure to make the life of the minorities a lot easier since they won't have to explain to foreigners that they are native Russians, but not ethnic Russians, etc. Such explanation will only make the point more muddled than it was before.

How They View Others and Each Other

The attitude of Russians to others depends a great deal upon who those others are. Their neighbours, without exception, are viewed as treacherous, mean, stingy and vile, and their prosperity is due to merciless exploitation of the Russians, their wits and natural resources. Were it not for the neighbours, Russia would now have been the envy of those proud Americans.

Americans were No. 1 enemy under the Communists, and this is why they are now looked upon with green-eyed envy, admiration and suspicion. Everybody knows that all Americans are incredibly rich, that even the beggars demand alms from the windows of their Mercedes. If only it were possible to work like Russians and to live like Americans.

The other Westerners are practically the same – they live in luxury and look down on the rest of the world, but with minor differences. The British are so amusing with their centuries-old traditions and silly sense of humour which nobody but themselves can understand. They are not too bad a people: they are relatives to the Czars and, like Russians, are very fond of tea. They have one author, Shakespeare. The French are all lovers, not one of them being true to his wife. Their author is Dumas, creator of *The Three Musketeers*. The Germans are seen as serious, studious, dull and hard-working. They read Schiller and quote Goethe. The last war with Germany is still looked upon with horror, but it was fought with other Germans. The Italians live in museums, eat pasta, drink Chianti and sing Neapolitan songs – very merry people. They have no authors, only lots of painters, sculptors and singers. Michelangelo and Pavarotti are the best.

The most enigmatic people are the Japanese. They are Orientals and as such should live like Russians or Indians or Chinese. The fact that they have a European standard of living is baffling, and most annoying. How can this be? Something must be terribly wrong with the Japanese – a mistake of nature.

Then there is the small problem of the other Russians. More and more (expatriate) Russians are fleeing to Russia from the countries which were formerly part of the Soviet Union. As the nation's birth rate is shrinking (at the present rate, by the mid-21st century there will be only half the number of Russians there are now), they are made welcome, but the local authorities are unpleasantly surprised by the fact that all of them expect a place to live and need jobs and salaries. Things are more complicated with real foreigners, like the Chinese and the Turks. The Chinese promote trade, but are spreading illegally all over the Russian Far East and changing the racial make-up of whole territories. Turks are employed as builders since it became clear that they do the job better and quicker than native Russians, much to the latter's indignation.

The people who are the butts of the Russians are the Chukchas, a tiny nation of meek and quiet people who live in the extreme north of the country, close relatives to American Indians. Why the Chukchas were chosen for this unenviable role is a mystery as there are scores of other minor nations in the country and Russians have no idea who any of them really are. Hardly any Russians have ever seen a living Chukcha. But you must admit that the very name sounds funny: Chuk-cha (chook-chah), and this is sufficient reason to laugh.

Jokes about Chukchas show them as gullible, simple-minded and incredibly dense people:

A Chukcha author is examined by a learned committee of distinguished Russian men of letters:
"Have you read anything by Tolstoy?"
"No."
"By Chekhov?"
"No."
"By Dostoyevsky?"
"No. Chukcha is not a reader. Chukcha is a writer!"

An armed Chukcha is guarding a military installation and sees a stranger coming. "Stop! I'll shoot!"
"I stop!"
"I shoot!"

The reason Russians enjoy those jokes may be that, deep inside, they see themselves in the Chukcha's shoes. For Chukcha is not a nation, it is a state of mind.

Character

Romantics at Heart

Scratch a Russian, and you will find a romantic. Russian romanticism is invincible, insuperable, unsinkable and unreasoning. A Russian sees havoc all around, sighs and looks hopefully round the corner: there must be success and happiness for all near at hand – it's in the newspapers.

The harder the life, the stronger the romantic in every Russian. How else could Communism have prevailed in this vast country? Russians thought that if a man worked according to his abilities, tomorrow or the day after he would receive according to the amount of labour donated to the common pot, and then everyone would get material and spiritual goods according to his needs... The Communist myth has now expired, but romanticism has stayed, and Russians happily believe their leaders who promise them paradise on earth.

A Feeling of Togetherness

The most characteristic feature of Russians is their feeling of togetherness. Imagine thousands of seals sunning themselves on a hard oceanic rock, so closely pressed against each other that it looks as if it is one big, black, gleaming beast. This is them, the Russians. Once you understand this, you understand what it is to be Russian, for there is hardly anything they may say or do that does not encompass this precious quality of togetherness.

This is why Russians love crowds. They would be devastated if one day they woke up to find that crowds had disappeared. A choosy Britisher will stop in disgust at the door of an overcrowded bus, and may even give it a miss; a Russian will energetically elbow his way on to the vehicle in which people are already packed like sawdust in Winnie-the-Pooh's round tummy. Once in, he will immediately ignore all the people who are squeezing the life out of him, comfortably settle himself down on his neighbour's corns, and may even manage to produce a newspaper from his overcoat and start to read.

Don't believe him if he complains about having to use the overcrowded vehicle. He is as fond of the dilapidated old dear, pickpockets and all, as an Englishman is of the old banger that has served him for an eternity and become part of himself. If things should ever change in the future, and vacant seats appear on the buses, he will sniff the air suspiciously and refuse to enter.

It was much easier for the Communist leaders to stuff Russian peasants into collective farms than, say, East German, Polish or Romanian ones. Unlike all those individualists, Russians were already partly prepared for shared work. Years of hard life had taught them that you can survive only if you can feel the shoulder of your neighbour. Collective farms may have been an idealistic concoction, but they survived in Russia for scores of years before failing miserably.

It would be hard to imagine a stiff Swede wholeheartedly joining in a cheerful chorus with complete strangers in a crowded train carriage. No vodka is needed to achieve this warm feeling of togetherness. The words do not matter and the tune may be completely ignored; what matters is the shrill pitch of roaring voices, the louder the better. We're together, so we're not afraid.

The Tortured Russian Soul

The Russian approach to life may be expressed with the help of three special concepts, *dusha*, *toska* and *sudjba*.

Dusha is soul, that enigmatic ethereal substance which only Russians are blessed with and which is inextricably bound up with Christian Orthodoxy. *Dusha* is the vital force in every living being; it is *dusha* that leaves one's body when one dies; it is your *dusha* that every demon is after.

Toska is a mixture of ennui, anguish, melancholy and boredom. It has been likened to the German *Weltschmerz*, but it is not quite that, being rather more personal. As a Russian, you should from time to time experience this unique emotion and complain loudly, like Pushkin's character, Eugene Onegin, in Tchaikovsky's opera: "What a shame! O my *toska*! O my wretched lot!"

Sudjba is an eclectic mixture of fortune, destiny, fate, lot and doom. 'You cannot escape your *sudjba*', 'If you fail, then such is your *sudjba*', etc. Your sacred duty is to bewail your wretched *sudjba* all your life.

It is not surprising that a Russian can change from being the life and soul of the company, clinking glasses and getting more outspoken by the hour, to a pitiful, maudlin figure who sobs over his drink and tortures himself about the meaning of life.

Bewailing your *sudjba* helps you not to forget that you live in hard times, that times have always been hard, and that the only change that may take place is for them to become worse. Any Russian, when asked, will tell you that in his youth things were so much better:

"Uncle Peter, when, in your opinion, was life better –
    under Khrushchev, or later, under Brezhnev?"
"Under Khrushchev, of course."
"But why, for goodness sake?"
"Women were younger then."

A Terrible Case of *Terpenie*

Another characteristic of the Russians is *terpenie*, a predisposition to long-suffering resignation: a passive and patient waiting till things get – or maybe don't get – better.

Russian *terpenie* appears inexhaustible:

The Government made up its mind to exterminate the Russians. It cut their salaries. The Russians did not utter a word. It made them homeless. The Russians stayed mute. At last, the frustrated authorities lost patience and ordered everyone to come to the main square. "Tomorrow each and every one of you is going to be hanged! Come at 8 a.m. sharp! Any questions?" "Yes. Shall we bring ropes ourselves, or will the Trade Union provide them?"

Russians are capable of waiting and hoping for the best under conditions that would seem unbearable for almost any other nation. Deep down they believe that *terpenie* and toil will overcome anything.

Attitudes and Values

The Bigger the Better

Russia is a huge country and its people like everything huge. Big is beautiful – gigantic river dams, gigantic tractor factories, gigantic nuclear rockets, gigantic television antennae. Size comes first, quality second. Dams on the Volga have turned the great river into a number of reservoirs polluted by the factories on its banks; nobody wants the bulky, clumsy, expensive tractors; the mighty Moscow TV mast burnt itself out and the firemen could do little about it; but the words 'the world's biggest' capture the imagination. They are balm to hurt Russian hearts. Bigger is better. Nothing can be more important than to be ahead of the rest of the world, in no matter what way.

In a well-known comic song, an African visitor criticizes Russia for her real and imaginary defects. Each criticism is answered by a patriotic Russian with the following refrain:

"Yes, but we also build nuclear rockets,
We have dammed the Yenisei river,
Besides, in the field of ballet
We're ahead of the whole world."

The Intelligentsia

The Russian intelligentsia is a population group of which no other nation has an equivalent. The intelligentsia should never be mixed up with intellectuals of which there are legion in every culture. Russians will never forgive you if you make this mistake.

"Do you know the difference between the intelligentsia and the rest?"
"Of course. If you are of the intelligentsia, you say 'Yes', and if not, 'Yep'."
"Thanks a lot. Are you yourself of the intelligentsia?"
"Yep."

If you are one of the intelligentsia, you should certainly be intelligent, but that is not enough. You should feel at one with your countrymen. You are compassionate, understanding and romantic, ready to raise your voice against injustice whenever necessary. You should also be cultured, educated and know how to behave. Not all authors, musicians, professors or academicians are recognized as belonging to the intelligentsia. Nor can you proclaim yourself to be one of the intelligentsia, just as you cannot declare that you are wise.

It is very flattering to be referred to as intelligentsia, though Lenin and other Bolsheviks always added the attribute 'rotten' to the term. In his works, Lenin (who came from a noble family and had a lawyer's degree) frequently associated the word 'intelligentsia' with 'shit'.

The intelligentsia is a sort of knightly order where members are named by popular vote. They are, by definition, opposed to any authority. If they ever have to admit that they share, or once shared, the government's view, they feel ashamed and hurry to explain that this is but an insignificant blip in their life story.

To Have and Have Not

Russians do not place much value on money. To have money is much better than to go without, for poverty is a great nuisance, but to have a lot of money is very bad form. Honest people cannot have a lot of money, not unless they are pop stars or tennis players. You should never boast that you have money; it is much better to complain that you cannot last from payday to payday without borrowing a few *roubles* from your next-door neighbour.

Rich people have always been heartily disliked. The New Russians, the nouveaux riches who have had their wealth thrust upon them all of a sudden, like a flower pot falling off the fifth-floor balcony, are an object of derision, e.g:

Two New Russians are dining at an elite restaurant. One of them throws a thick wad of *roubles* to the waiter and says magnanimously: "Keep the change!"

Not wishing to be outdone, the other New Russian approaches the cloakroom and, throwing his ticket to attendant, says airily: "Keep the coat!"

If you earn very little, there is absolutely nothing wrong in letting others know how much, or, rather, how little, you earn, because admitting that you are grossly underpaid says only that your employer does not understand what a priceless acquisition he made when he hired you. It is not humiliating to earn little – the blame falls on the head of the person who exploits you.

The pitiful looking beggars at every street corner demonstrating their missing limbs and asking for alms are seldom ignored. It is rumoured that some of them often do well enough to go home by taxi, which costs rather more than an average worker can afford.

Russians are ready to help others even if they know that the man they are helping could help himself. In olden days, peasants would leave a piece of bread and a cup of milk outside their door at night in case a runaway convict passed by. It might be the very man who burgled your home a year ago, but today he is among the unlucky ones. 'Don't be too sure that you, too, won't one day go to prison or go a-begging', the proverb says. Besides, you can't be certain that the man has been sentenced for a real crime, because you know what the government is capable of.

You can never tell if young Russians are rich or poor by their clothes for they may have spent their last pennies on their jeans or latest tie or trainers with a famous label (Western, of course). Being well dressed is very prestigious in Russia, and every dandy of both sexes is measured by the clothes he or she wears. It is different with older people. Youngsters may and should dress well, but old pepper-pots should know their place. It is almost indecent when an elderly lady or, still worse, man is dressed in the latest fashion. What does the old fool think he is? A gigolo?

String Pulling

'You scratch my back and I'll scratch yours.' The equivalent proverb in Russia may use different words – 'One hand washes another' – but the meaning is much the same.

When you start a new venture, the first thing you must do is find the right person to help you. Ideally, it should be a relative, or someone who owes you a favour. Once found, everything else is easy because he in his turn has friends. "I'll send a load of bricks to the construction site of your summer house, and you'll ask the examiners to be lenient towards my lazybones of a son who wants to go to university." It is nothing to do with bribery. Not a *rouble* is involved. It's *blat* ('a' is read as 'u' in 'cup'), the most powerful weapon Russia has ever known, a master key that opens all doors. You do a favour for someone, not for money, but in the expectation of the day that you may need his services. If there is one system in Russia which works like clockwork, it's *blat*.

Signs of Superstition

Russians are fairly superstitious. A black cat crossing your path cannot be ignored; be careful not to spill salt or break a mirror; if you're going to an examination, don't forget to slip a coin into your shoe...

A small monument to a hare honours the one that crossed Pushkin's path in 1825 when the poet was on his way to St Petersburg to join an uprising against the Czarist regime. Seeing the hare, he ordered the sledge to turn back. But for superstition, he would have ended his days in the Siberian coal mines.

The latest fascination is with the Oriental calendar. At the start of the Chinese New Year, Russians excitedly ask each other whose year it is – Tiger, Ox, Horse, Monkey. Even a sensible woman will declare in all seriousness that since she was born in the Year of the Rat and her star sign is Pisces, she cannot marry a particular man because his animal and his sign can never be happy with hers. Yet she will insist she is a true Orthodox Christian and will regularly light candles in her parish church.

Divine Faith

Before the Bolshevik take-over, Russia was a God-fearing country where thousands of pilgrims marched from one monastery to another on a never-ending tour because the

17

number of holy places was so immense.

The Communists put a quick end to all this. Churches were destroyed, the priests were shot or sent to Siberia, and atheism reigned supreme. During this time if someone admitted he was a believer, or much worse a church-goer, it was a sign that he didn't care about his job. With the ending of Communist rule, Russians discovered much to their chagrin that without religion there seemed very little in life to hold to. A complete turnaround followed, and they laid all their hopes at the church's door. Needless to say, this hasn't got them very far.

In spite of the decades of Communism, Russians are still on the whole a religious lot, though this doesn't mean that large numbers attend church. In fact, the time is rapidly approaching when parishes will fight one another for their flock.

The thousand-year-old Russian Orthodox branch of Christianity is opposed to all the other branches, above all to Roman Catholicism and Protestantism. Orthodox Russians think they are the only true believers and that there is absolutely no hope of salvation for anyone else.

In fact, even infidel Muslims are considered better than those Western dissenters from the faith of the forefathers. Strange though it might seem, for all their religious differences, Tartars and Mongols (who as Russians are taught at school were once their cruel oppressors) are treated either in a friendly way or with indifference, while Christians in the West are looked upon with suspicion and distrust. The explanation is that Catholic Christians' favourite figure from the Scriptures is the active and efficient Apostle Peter, while Russians would rather side with the wise philosopher John the Divine (of *Revelations*). It's a division that illustrates the main difference in the national character of Russians and Westerners.

Ancient churches in Russia are part of the nation's cultural pride, and many of the thousands that were ruined under Communism are being restored. In almost all of them, on the Western gallery wall there is an impressive fresco of the Last Judgement in which sinners in Oriental turbans and Pilgrim Father type tall hats are obediently walking into the eternal flames where abominable looking devils are ready to torture them, while saints clad in Russian style garb are welcomed by the benevolent Apostle Peter jingling his keys of Paradise. The frescos prove that all but Russian Orthodox believers will burn in hell.

Family Matters

The Ruler of the Roost

Power in Russia has been in the hands of women for a long time. Russian feminists never needed to declare war on men, since men freely surrendered to the more educated, more cultured, more intelligent, more hard-working, less hard-drinking sex. In relatively unimportant fields, such as politics, men still prevail, but amongst teachers, doctors, engineers, not to mention service staff, as well as families, woman reigns supreme. If the husband is the head of the family, the wife is the neck, dictating which way the head will look. Defeated and subdued, Russian men submissively, and it seems almost willingly, bow to 'the weaker sex'.

It is not for nothing that, grammatically, 'Russia' has the feminine gender. She is Mother Russia – nobody would dream of calling her 'Father'.

The Shrinking Family

There is a big gap between belief and reality in Russian family life. Ask a Russian about his values, and he will tell you that above all he values his family and children.

What is more, he honestly believes he is speaking the truth. He will probably tell you that family connections are propped up by the ancient rule of name-giving. If you are Nikolai and your father was Boris, the only way of politely addressing you will be Nikolai Borisovich, i.e. Nikolai, son of Boris. Let Brazilians squeeze the names of their favourite football team, reserve included, between the first and the last names of their offspring. The Russian son of Boris is Borisovich, and that's that.

Yet divorces are quickly outnumbering marriages, and a family with one child, or even with none, is more typical than a family with two or three. Children may be the flowers of life, but let them grow under the neighbour's window. Children have become too expensive, especially if you take into consideration that your child simply cannot be dressed worse than the Ivanovs next door, and giving him an education is ruinous to your budget because you don't want your little precious to go to the state school round the corner. It will cost a pretty penny, sending him off to a private school, but what won't you do for your Only One?

With a single child in the family, Russian parents heap the heavy weight of their love on the poor, innocent head of their offspring, a love which in former times would have been shared among innumerable siblings.

The Benevolent *Babushka*

The person who really spares the rod and thus spoils the child is *babushka*, the grandmother.

Having reached retirement age, which in Russia is 55, she immediately throws out her make-up, forgets the name of her hairdresser, casts off all her more or less wearable clothes and dons an old padded coat that her late granddad wore when he went winter fishing. Together with a pair of rubber boots, it makes a fine outfit, perfectly good for taking care of her beloved grand-child. The child's mother can be certain that nothing will happen to the child while she is out working: *Babushka* will see to it that he has everything he wants, and much more. If Daddy or Mummy say "No" to the young master's whim, he knows that if he goes to Grandma, she will always say "Yes". The mother's first baby is her last doll. The grandmother's first grandchild is her first baby.

In Russia the elderly have always been shown respect, especially if they are your own relatives. The most ignominious thing you can do is send your decrepit mother or father to a home. Old folks' homes in Russia are insti-tutions of the lowest reputation, and it is well deserved. Each generation is taught to show respect to their elders, and every child is told to give up his seat on a bus to the elderly (seats are also reserved for the disabled and moth-ers with babies). The fact that this practice has all but died out hasn't stopped them from being told to do it. It's considered an absolute must.

The Generation Gap

It is hardly surprising that the generation gap is very wide in Russia. In all those countries which were part of the Soviet Union it is wider than anywhere else. The rapid change in the social system could not but produce an entire generation that has never known the calamities its forebears went through. It is only in films that the young see war, concentration camps and long bread lines. They can say what they like, and nobody will bother to report them to the secret police. They can leave the country without difficulty and then come back. They can marry a foreigner and do even worse things, like listening and dancing to Western music. For their grandparents, who have the chance to do all this only at the sunset of their lives, such things are incredible and not always desirable.

21

Youngsters smile when the old ones start their usual "When I was your age...", for the ages are so different that no comparison seems possible.

The last generation to live under Communist rule now divides into two groups: those who welcome the changes and those who are nostalgic about times past. The latter have forgotten the hard times and remember the days when their future was bleak but assured, when they did not have to compete for a job or a career. They would do anything to bring back the days when, as a Russian comedian told it, you got your modest wage of 120 *roubles* if you made numerous bicycles at your factory, 120 *roubles* if you made few bicycles, and the same sum if you made no bicycles at all. Nobody needed those blasted bicycles, anyway, they were made of rotten stuff, but you got your wages all the same.

Medical services were totally inadequate, but free; education was of poor quality but you never paid a *kopek*, even for university. The army ate up most of the country's budget, but it was the most powerful army in the world and everyone was afraid of Russia. Those who remember find it strange that today's young are indifferent to all those splendours of life under socialism, when you could bang your shoe on the UN rostrum, or explode a couple of experimental A-bombs in the Far North, just to show the world who was who.

Manners

To say that Russians don't have any manners in the Western sense of the word is to do them an injustice. They do have some, it's just that they are different.

Where an over-polite Japanese will probably say 'Would you be so kind as to do it in such a way that the window should find itself open?' and an Englishman will limit himself to 'Could you please open the window?', the Russian, with brisk economy, will say no more than the curt "Open the window, please", which saves a lot of time and effort.

What constitutes proper behaviour is a soft voice, a quiet gait, and clothes that are not too loud. There is no reticence about expressing your feelings in public; for instance, if you are displeased with the service in a shop or a restaurant, you can tell the shop assistant or the waiter exactly what you think of him, his relatives, his in-laws, his habits and his sexual bias. But fist fighting in public is not approved, so when it happens there will always be someone who will pull the protagonists apart. A Russian may even start a fight in the expectation that someone will stop him. "Hold me, people, before I spread this son-of-a-gun against the wall!"

When meeting, men kiss each other on both cheeks if they are friends and have not seen each other for ages. Three kisses are due if both are clergymen or one of them is Brezhnev. Not long ago, young people who kissed in public would be taken off to the police station. Passers-by would blush and turn away in shame. Now you may even kiss a policeman and nobody would mind, including the policeman: this is how far Russians have gone in imitating the manners of the corrupted West.

On entering their homes, Russians take off their shoes and put on slippers. Housewives keep a few extra pairs of slippers for guests. This is because even in cities the streets may not be paved, and if any asphalt does exist, it looks as if it has been churned up by a small tank detachment. Moreover, as it is not frowned on to drop litter in the streets and the miserable wages of the street sweepers do not encourage more than a lazy swing of their brooms, shoes can't help but carry dirt to your door.

In the days when standing in line occupied a considerable part of Russian life a special queuing etiquette developed

23

with its own rules and taboos, like no queue jumping, and not leaving the line for a long time. Now that the shops are full of goods and the only problem is where to get money to buy them, many a housewife secretly hankers for those long hours of waiting, when you enjoyed the company of others: good company is good company.

As a substitute, modern Russian women use benches at the entrance to their blocks of flats. You will see the gossips solemnly sitting there, watching people come and go and exchanging the latest news of their courtyard. You can rely on them if you want to know if Tania Manina had a visitor today, or if Mania Tanina has changed her boyfriend.

A Salutary Address

Like an English parson, Russians use 'thou' when speaking with God, but whereas the parson sticks to 'you' with everybody else, Russians 'thou' a lot more people – their parents, close relatives, best friends (and sometimes enemies, to show how much they despise them). If Russians begin a heated discussion with '*Vy*' (vee) and then, at some crucial point, change it for '*ty*' (tee), this signifies an abrupt severance of diplomatic relations.

Your parents are always '*ty*', for why should you be extra polite with people who have to put up with you whatever happens? On the other hand, when lovers abandon the polite '*Vy*' and enter a '*ty*' relationship, it means that an intimate change has taken place.

Words of address, like Sir and Madam, do not exist in Russia, which gives Russians a lot of discomfort. Before the Bolshevik Revolution of 1917, the normal salutation was *Sudarj* for a man and *Sudarinya* for a woman. The words were bourgeois and were anathema to revolutionary democrats who suggested *Grazhdanin* (Citizen), as in the days of the French revolution, or *Tovarishch*

(Comrade). Unfortunately, 'Citizen' was associated with law and order rather than with everyday relations. *Tovarishch* was a Communist Party word but after the fall of the Communists, those who did not think much of past times would not use it, and they were the overwhelming majority. As *Sudarj* sounded hopelessly outdated, the situation looked and still is insoluble.

If you know the person's surname, you can always use *Gospodin* Ivanov or *Gospozha* Ivanova (i.e. Mr and Mrs Ivanov), but this is rather formal. In despair, many Russians have turned to the simple 'Man' and 'Woman' but others refuse to accept these and see them as vulgar. A temporary solution is to use the Russian version of the English 'Excuse me', and avoid addressing the person at all.

Obsessions

In the last years of Communist rule the scarcity of food prompted the saying that a Russian woman had two obsessions: where to get food and how to lose weight. The paradox had a simple explanation. There may have been no food on the shop counter, but there was certain to be some under it, and if you were a friend of the shop assistant... well, who wasn't in those days? In fact, few people really starved, but getting good food was always a problem of time, extra money and a lot of grovelling.

A popular rhyme claimed that only four people in Russia had the prime of everything: the salesgirl Nyurka, Gagarin Yurka, German Titov and Nikita Khrushchev. (Yuri Gagarin and German Titov were, of course, the first Soviet cosmonauts.)

Changing times have modified the obsessions. Losing weight is still a big problem for both sexes, while looking for food has given way to looking for good food at a cheaper price. Really good food means large chunks of meat, potatoes, pasta, lots of bread and heaps of home-made jam. Cholesterol? What's cholesterol?

Drinking and Eating

Drinking is much more important for a Russian than eating. Russia is a drinking country. One thousand years ago, when the heathen Eastern Slavs were considering which new religion to choose, Prince Vladimir rejected Islam for the sole reason that Muslims shun alcohol. "The joy of Russia is drinking!" declared the worthy Prince and was consequently proclaimed Equal-to-the-Apostles by grateful compatriots.

The chief national drink is vodka. Russians have three kinds of money – *roubles*, dollars and vodka, the latter serving as currency when you pay a plumber, or hire a tractor driver to plough your vegetable plot. People certainly prefer to be paid in vodka rather than *roubles* because vodka may be drunk the moment you get your hands on it without the tedious procedure of going to the wine shop, to say nothing of having to explain to your wife where the money went. Every sensible old country woman keeps a few bottles of vodka under her bed to be made use of when the time comes for planting the pota-toes or to getting her well cleaned.

Vodka is also the chief tool in starting a conversation. Do not forget to take along a bottle when going to visit a Russian. If you sit at the table across from him, look him in the eye and say nothing, he will suspect you of making a pass at him. But once a bottle appears between you, mutual understanding is immediately established. If there is one thing Russians hate more than anything else, it is drinking alone. (This is only seen at the last stage on the road to delirium tremens.) A sober Russian will always look for company when he feels a dire need to wet his whistle. Scores of bars in every town or city provide the perfect place to sit, to drink, to smoke, to dance and, with luck, to punch a nose or two.

The normal number of people taking part in a drinking session is three. There are serious reasons for this. Firstly, it is cheaper, since you will not always have enough money for a whole bottle. Secondly, there are approximately three big glassfuls of vodka in one half-litre bottle, and one glass as a rule is sufficient to help you feel carefree and merry. Thirdly, it is so much more interesting to have an animated discussion when there are three of you. Lastly, who will make peace if two of you get engaged in a discussion too heated for words alone?

Special feasts simply cannot be enjoyed without drink – vodka for men, vodka and wine for women – in unbelievable quantities. Russians will express concern and sympathy if you refuse a glass or two, because the only thing it can mean is that you are seriously ill. If you do not care for vodka, the only acceptable excuse will be that you have an ulcer or cancer.

Beer production and consumption is on the rise. Beer is best when you have it with *vobla* (Caspian roach), a small, heavily salted, dried fish which is so hard that before you can bite into it you have to take it by the tail and beat it savagely against the edge of the table. The more you eat of it, the thirstier you become and the more beer you need to consume.

Tramps make very good money collecting empty bottles, and the morning after a festive holiday they could well make a fortune. They would, if they did not hurry to drink the money they receive as soon as the last bottle on their territory has been collected and handed in at special tents where bottle collection is organized on a large scale.

In rural areas people do not normally have to buy drink as moonshining provides the necessary. The liquid

27

usually tastes abominable, but this never stops an experienced drinker. Government efforts to curb heavy drinking and make Russian society a bit more sober are doomed to failure. Drinking prowess is a matter of pride. To drink a lot without getting really drunk is the secret wish of every Russian. This is why Boris Yeltsin was referred to as 'our man', a true Russian, his drunken escapades evoking friendly laughter rather than indignation.

Hearty Appetites

On the whole, Russians go for quantity. They are hearty eaters, and the word 'diet' is Greek to most of them. If an Englishman invites you for afternoon tea, you will get a cup of very good tea, possibly accompanied by a small biscuit. If a Russian invites you for tea, don't ever eat before visiting. On your arrival you will see a table bending under the weight of food. There is no worse disaster for a Russian host than if all the food is eaten up by the guests. Better by far is to have half the food left over, a clear sign that your friends could not devour more. Of course, this means that you will have to live on leftovers for a week, but that is the only drawback to an otherwise successful occasion.

The Russian national dish is *kasha*, thick cooked grain or groats – very tasty and nutritious. Buckwheat *kasha* is the king, delicious with milk. Milk products are popular, especially *smetana*, roughly translated as sour milk cream.

There is hardly a dish which Russians would eat without a large slice of bread – you just cannot feel fed if there is no bread on the table.

Russians eat three meals a day – breakfast, a midday meal and an evening meal – but few people are satisfied with this austere arrangement so take regular snacks. Breakfast can be anything from bread to *kasha* or pasta, always with a lot of tea. The overwhelming majority prefer bread, as usually there isn't time in the morning to prepare anything else. Some people drink coffee, but its popularity is severely curtailed by its price. Tea is not cheap either, but Russians cannot imagine life without it, and every housewife is proud of her own way of making good tea which she learnt from her great-grandmother.

The heaviest meal is taken in the middle of the day. Soup is an absolute must. If there is no soup, then it's not a meal, it's a snack. Russian soups have absolutely nothing in common with those funny-looking substances offered in the West in tiny bowls. Russians demand large platefuls of hot soup, cooked with cabbage, beetroot, potatoes, carrots and onions, with a huge chunk of meat arrogantly displayed in the middle of the dish and a generous portion of *smetana*. This is Russian Soup. Once you have tasted it, you will never again eat anything else called soup other than Russian.

Before the soup there is an appetizer such as mixed fresh vegetables served in a huge bowl with sunflower seed oil or *smetana*. The soup is followed by a dish which must include a good portion of meat or fish accompanied by *kasha*, pasta, potatoes or other boiled vegetables. After this tea or coffee is served with a sweet biscuit. Having swallowed all this, a Russian either crawls back to work and sleeps the rest of the day in his office chair, or, if he is at home, spreads his tired limbs on a sofa and covers his face with a newspaper.

The evening meal looks very much like the midday meal but without the soup. So naturally you get hungry by bedtime, and to go to sleep on an empty stomach is unthinkable. So there is one more meal, secret and therefore wisely unnamed but nevertheless quite substantial, after which the Russian slaps himself on his visibly expanded belly and goes to bed, sufficiently content. Before falling asleep, he may watch television where he will learn that winter food shortages may be imminent because food consumption has assumed threatening proportions.

29

The table on feast days and holidays differs from the everyday one, not only because of the quantity of food displayed but also its diversity. A large number of things are consumed only on special occasions. There might be black and red caviar, or pickled or smoked fish or mushrooms of all kinds. In Russian forests delectable mushrooms are found in abundance.

Russians eat tons of jam. In autumn there can be a serious shortage of sugar in the shops as every housewife hurries to make use of cheap fruit and fill all the jars she can find with apple jam, cherry jam, plum jam, strawberry jam. It is good manners for guests to taste their hostess's jam, express admiration and ask for the recipe, of which there are millions.

As for snacks, at every corner you can buy little pies fried in boiling oil. Small shoemaker's nails are said to be considerably more harmful to the stomach but easier to extract. The taste of both is similar.

Health and Hygiene

The Russians' main health problem is alcoholism and its associated problems such as heart disease and pancreatitis. Drink-related diseases are closely followed by those caused by smoking, which affect women as much as men. The average life expectancy for Russian men is 61, and for women 73.

Doctors in Russia bear very little resemblance to their Western colleagues. To begin with they are all women, there are a great many of them, and they are grossly underpaid. To make ends meet, doctors have to have several jobs which certainly adds to their experience in how to treat several patients at once.

Health services in Russia are officially free, which is a

blessing and a curse. If you want a quick consultation you should probably go to your local doctor; but if you have a serious problem it is better to visit a paid specialist. Ironically, when you see the latter you may well recognize the familiar face of the former. Sometimes the former and the latter are not only the same person, but they will see you in the same consulting room.

A Russian who has his teeth fixed or replaced in Russia can never work as a spy in the West for he will immediately be exposed by his steel or gold crowns as soon as he opens his mouth.

Richer Russians unpatriotically prefer to be treated abroad. However, quite a lot of foreigners visit Russia to get treatment from famous Russian opthalmologists or paediatricians or surgeons. It is another manifestation of Russian *terpenie* that specialists of world renown accept working at home for a paltry salary rather than going abroad to establish a clinic and earn more money. If this is not patriotism, what is?

All Steamed Up

To a Russian visiting a bath-house (both Russian-style and sauna) is not so much hygiene as sheer sensual delight, the greatest pleasure possible in this world and the next. Russian prudery won't allow both sexes in the same bath-house, but otherwise it is both very different from the luxury of Roman baths and very close in its social function. It is a place to sit and sweat, to drink beer and talk politics, to relax, to play chess and to collect your thoughts. In a Russian bath-house the steam room is equivalent to a medieval torture chamber. You don't sweat there, you are mercilessly dehydrated and to make matters still more satisfying you are beaten with a besom made of leafy birch or better still oak twigs.

When even the strongest helplessly drops unconscious

to the floor in a heap, a bucket of ice-cold water is thrown over his lifeless but still steaming body. This is a signal that he is supposed to get up and walk, on shaky legs, into the washroom where he sluices his body down and then goes to the cooler changing-room which is also a sort of sitting-room, where, wrapped in a sheet, he may enjoy a beer or discuss politics with another masochist. After a time, he will dress and very slowly walk home, his personal besom under arm, his red-hot face gleaming with pleasure and contentment.

In small country bath-houses in villages, instead of a bucket of cold water you may jump out naked and plunge into the river or roll in the snow, depending on the season. It's supposed to be good for the nervous system.

Russians with less will-power and with more self-pity prefer milder forms of exercise, such as fitness clubs, swimming and tennis. Joggers are rare, probably because they are afraid of the sneers of passers-by who would very much like to join them but find the role of critical onlooker a lot less onerous. It's a perfect way to preserve one's self-esteem.

A Full-bodied Account

If you meet a Russian in the street and are thoughtless enough to ask him how things are, he will stop, take one or two deep breaths, and start to tell you in torrid detail. He will list all his and his wife's ills, and what happened when he followed the doctor's advice; you will learn how he feels today; you will be told how his younger son is doing at school, and what the teacher had to say when he telephoned her last night.

Never, ever ask a Russian how things are – that is, unless you are truly interested in whether or not his bowels moved this morning.

Sense of Humour

The Russian sense of humour is poignant and rough, often rude and obscene. Where the British will respond to something funny with a thin condescending smile, Russians will roar with laughter.

A woman with a dog is getting into a taxi. The taxi driver asks without turning,
"Where shall we take this bitch?"
"It's not a bitch. It's a male dog."
"I'm not talking to you."

Hundreds of years of oppression and censorship in Russia have given birth to a special folk genre, that of the political joke, or *anekdot*, which, being oral, was able to develop uncensored. In spite of the frantic efforts of the KGB, or Secret Police, the *anekdot* flourished throughout the 70-odd years of Soviet power, though if caught telling or even listening to some of those jokes, you could get up to ten years in a concentration camp. As times got easier, a devaluation of jokes occurred, and an *anekdot* worth ten years in camp went for only five. For instance:

Brezhnev hears the doorbell, comes to the front door, puts on his glasses, pulls out a piece of paper and carefully reads: "Who's there?" His close associate at the other side of the door does the same and reads: "It's me, Comrade Podgorny."

In another version, nobody answers Brezhnev's question. When, after repeating it, he opens the door to see who it is, there's Podgorny. "Why didn't you answer when I asked?" "I've left my piece of paper at home."

Such jokes are still popular, though with the advent of more relaxed times the satirical sting has become considerably less sharp. When the Iron Curtain was raised and people were allowed to communicate with foreigners, the

Russians viewed the living conditions of Westerners with amazement. Jokes became self-deprecatory:

A Western worker is showing a Russian colleague his house. "This is my room, this is my wife's, that one is my elder daughter's, that one is our dining-room, then comes the guest room," etc., etc. The Russian nods and says, after a moment's hesitation, "Well, I've got more or less the same. Only without the partitions."

After the complete failure of all the so-called reforms introduced by former Communists who thought more about their own than the nation's prosperity, people revived the old Russian saying that there are two major calamities in Russia: fools and (impassable) roads. One more calamity has been added to the saying which now goes: 'There are fools, roads, and fools who tell us which road to take.'

Russians are unsurpassed in the masochistic skill of being able to laugh at oneself:

One Russian, a drunk; two Russians, a fist fight; three Russians, a local Communist party unit. One Englishman, a gentleman; two Englishmen, a bet; three Englishmen, a parliament. One Frenchman, a lover; two Frenchmen, a duel; three Frenchmen, a revolution. One Jew, a shop; two Jews, an international chess tournament; three Jews, a Russian State Symphony Orchestra.

The story of Russia is the story of a permanent war between Ignorance and Injustice.

The severity of Russian laws is moderated by the optional nature of their execution.

Like every other nation, Russia has its kings of comedy. Almost all of them dwell on political problems and economic difficulties. At their performances, the tongue-tied politicians, the crooks and the big-time swindlers laugh the loudest.

The *enfant terrible* of Russian comedians is Victor Shenderovich with his weekly television political review *Itogo* (Altogether) and the nationwide show *Kookly* (The Puppets), the Russian version of *Spitting Image*. The Russian puppets are technically far more sophisticated and more easily recognizable. Watching the show gives one a rare feeling of being personally involved in the absurd atmosphere of the Kremlin's intrigues and dismal failures. No politician is spared, and the sting is merciless, sometimes almost too cruel to be funny. The President and his immediate retinue are the usual objects of derision. Kremlin leaders may be infuriated, but there is little they can do, officially that is. Russians have every reason to suspect that the most senior political figures have serious problems with their sense of humour. This is very un-Russian.

Systems

No system works normally in Russia. The idiosyncrasies of buses, trams and trains are the talk of every town. If an intercity train arrives on time, it's sure to be in the papers next morning. If you are lucky, you get your morning post by 4 p.m., which is also the time of the evening post. A lot depends on the mood of the post-woman or whether she has already taken her child to the kindergarten and done her shopping.

Taken for a Ride

But to look on the bright side, public transport allows one to get to every corner of the city, or the country for that matter. The fares are low, and besides, at least four out of five Russians ride free: the pensioners, the police, civil servants, army personnel – there are few who have not been taken care of by the thoughtful law-makers. As a rule the small number of unprivileged do not buy tickets either; they would rather be fined once in a while than suffer the ignominy of having to pay for the ride.

The few Russian cities that have a metro are justly proud of this unusually efficient means of transport. In Communist times the metro was meant to serve as a showcase of the country's victorious socialism and a lot of effort (and money) was spent to this effect, not without good results.

With prices of plane tickets soaring higher than the planes, the railway provides the chief method of transport in the vast Russian expanses. If you want an idea of how huge Russia is, take a trans-Siberian train which will carry you across the country, through Siberia and the Far Eastern Russian provinces, down to the shores of the Sea of Japan – the journey lasting about ten days. It will take you a whole day to pass by Lake Baikal alone. According to Siberian Russians, in Siberia 100 years is no real age, 100 kilometres is no real distance, 100 millilitres of vodka is no real drink. Indeed, as far as distance and drink are concerned, they will say these figures are an understatement and that they should be multiplied by at least five.

When the first Russian railways were being laid, the wise strategists decided that the Russian railway gauge should be made slightly different from the Western one, to prevent enemy trains from bringing in troops and ammunition. Somehow it never entered their scheming heads that the difficulty would be mutual. From that time on Russian trains have been doomed to the long and tiresome process of changing the wheel units each time the train crosses the national border. All the newly formed states, part of the former Russian Empire, and the Soviet Union are hampered by the same problem. Sometimes it is difficult to rid oneself of the impression that Russians are very good at creating problems and then heroically overcoming them.

A number of good roads and motorways exist, but in many cases unmade roads are a test of endurance, especially after heavy rain.

Every city in Russia has zebra crossings adorning its streets. They look very modern and certainly demonstrate the country's unswerving path to progress and adherence to Western values. But if you step on to one in sight of a moving vehicle, you are clearly suffering from suicidal tendencies.

A Bit of a Squeeze

The centres of old Russian cities are usually a joy to the eye – a delightful assortment of epochs, styles and designs. Visitors and photographers love them, but the citizens who live in the old dilapidated houses and those who are responsible for their upkeep hate them. Every ancient house that crumbles away from years of neglect raises an outcry among lovers of architectural heritage and a sigh of relief on the part of the authorities.

The newer areas of Russian cities look quite different. Most urban Russians live in big blocks of flats many storeys high. Those built after the Second World War look like gigantic dominoes, either vertical or horizontal. Each flat has a balcony, often glazed by the owner to suit his own taste and particular sense of beauty, which turns the original ugly structure into something repulsively original. Whole cities are built in this way, dismal and monotonous, though as modern conveniences, they serve their purpose.

Quite another matter is that people are squeezed into these buildings like herrings in a barrel. They live in microscopic flats; if two people meet in the passage, one of them has to back up. The lavatories are so narrow that a person of more than medium weight has one more reason to think of dieting. Cupboards are rare, and for many families buying a washing machine is a two-fold problem; expense, and where to put it when you get it. People joke that, to save space, a new invention is needed: a chamber pot with the handle on the inside.

Sometimes two families share a bathroom and a kitchen. Two people living in a three-room apartment is an unthinkable luxury. It's foolish to ask a Russian how many bedrooms he has, as there aren't any. Each room serves all purposes, so instead of beds people tend to sleep on sofas or divans easily transformed into whatever-you-like-at-the-moment. Yet due to their feeling of togetherness, Russians do not suffer in this situation as much as an outsider might think. One of the most popular Russian proverbs runs: 'Better for everyone to be crammed in than for anyone to be left out.'

The kitchen is minute. In new flats it is so small that a table and fridge hardly leave elbow room for the busy housewife. Yet somehow the whole family manages to have their regular meals there and often, when the children are in bed and must not be disturbed, the rest of the family and even visiting friends meet round the kitchen table with a bottle of vodka. The kitchen was even more popular in Soviet times, when the intelligentsia gathered there in heated political discussions lasting far into the small hours of the night. Sometimes those discussions ended in concentration camps.

Communal services in Russia are usually so poor that everyone needs to be able to do plumbing and wallpapering, to build bookshelves, replace electrical wiring, whitewash the ceiling, paint the floor, and so on. In fact, all Russia is a huge Do-It-Yourself arena. If you feel that a repair is beyond your capabilities, you can always ask the plumber or electrician who lives next door. He will come immediately (if he is sober). Applying to the building's manager will take much more time and effort, and the result may not be worth the trouble.

Country Life

A Russian peasant hut looks very much like a log cabin on a Christmas greeting card, only better. The wooden window decorations remind you of exquisite lace and the sills are crowded with flowering plants. Each cabin is surrounded by a kitchen garden or an orchard, which adds to the idyll.

Inside it is not quite so picturesque. The rooms can be quite dim since much of the light is stolen by the flowers sitting on the window-sills. But then why should you want a lot of light if most of your time you spend in the open? It's a chance to give your eyes a rest.

The greater part of the biggest room is occupied by a huge Russian stove, a very useful and cleverly designed multi-purpose brick structure, fed with wood. You cook on the stove, you bake in the stove, the house is heated by it and you sleep on its flat top.

Running water in a peasant hut is rare. To use the 'outhouse', as the name suggests, necessitates having to go out into the yard – a fairly unpleasant experience in winter when it's minus 30 degrees.

Russian peasants are a peculiar lot. Active in warm seasons, they all but hibernate in the long winter. There is not much you can do when the ground is waist-deep in snow. Their two best companions, which help them wile away the monotony, are the television and a bottle of *samogon*, home-made spirit mostly distilled from sugar. When there is no sugar, you can use corn or sugar beet – in fact, there's hardly anything you cannot use.

It's all different in summer, when there is land to be ploughed, vegetable plots to be weeded, fodder to be produced (with luck, the source of the fodder might well be the nearby collective farm where the guard is your close relative). Under the Communists, you could only keep one cow; now you may have as many as your cowshed can hold. On a collective farm, a cow that can yield

3,000 litres of milk a year is a record holder, the pride of the herd; on a private peasant holding it is much more, though never as much as in Holland or Denmark where no-one is surprised by 10,000 litres.

Collective farms are dying out, as is the Russian village as such. The young flock to the cities, while older folk look forward to their retirement years. But in summer, village life is quite lively when sons and daughters come from the cities to enjoy the fresh air, to pick mushrooms and to swim in the river. They often bring the children, much to the joy of the village *babushkas* who can indulge themselves to their heart's content scolding and spoiling.

The Bare Necessities

A problem arises every year that completely baffles the Russian authorities. This is that after the hot summer comes autumn, which is followed by the cold winter, which, in turn, will quite unexpectedly give way to spring. Every change of season is met with a surprised "Ah!" and the unpleasant discovery that nobody is prepared for the change. For instance, in winter there may be no fuel: it was sold to buy seeds which were sold to buy fertilizer which somehow never reached the farms, and the official responsible indifferently shrugs his shoulders and says, "What can I do? I am new here, it's only my third year of service." His predecessor was dismissed three years ago for not lifting a finger.

Fortunately, the Russians' *terpenie* means that they can survive anything, from hurricanes and floods to months-long periods of cold stoves and no electricity when the temperature outside is well below freezing. To stay alive in extreme conditions one needs warm clothes and a good store of spirits. Russians know this only too well, and providently stock up on these necessities long before the arrival of the first snow flurries.

Educational Excellence

Russian teachers observe a considerably higher educational standard in schools compared with many similar institutions in the West. Russian students often win prizes at all sorts of international competitions.

Schooling begins with kindergarten. Russian kindergartens are special establishments with their own buildings and staff where little Russian hopefuls gradually learn the difference between home and the outer world. Real school – Monday to Saturday – begins when children are six or seven years old. An experiment to let schoolchildren stay at home on Saturdays rapidly fizzled out as many parents work on Saturdays and not everyone has a *babushka* to take care of the children. In any case, who wants to have demanding young at home when after a hard working week you need a day to catch up? After all, Saturday is also a day for washing and shopping and cleaning the house.

All over Russia children work with the same books and follow one curriculum. If your parents suddenly make up their minds to move from Murmansk in the north to Vladivostok in the extreme east, you can take your school books with you in the knowledge that over there at that very moment your year is also doing simple fractions.

This practical state of affairs is coming to an end however, as more and more new school books on the same subject appear to differ from each other. Childbirth may be on the decrease, but the number of educational authors is steadily increasing. The desired goal is evidently to give each child his own original textbook.

There is one small drawback to this otherwise perfect Russian school system of serious teachers, hard work, lots of homework and endless cramming: the children hate it. Happily, in summer they get their reward by being packed off to camps. Throughout the three-month-long vacation one can see crowds of excited children and parents gathering in some park or railway square, heavily loaded with bags and knapsacks. In Communist days, the camps were called Pioneer Camps, with sham-military parades, horn-blowing, morning line-ups, etc. Now the young have a lot more freedom, with excursions, walking tours and, of course, discos. Much of the expense of going to camp is paid by the factories and workplaces where the parents are employed.

In cities, most children go to the nearest school a few blocks from home, which means that there is no need for school buses. But if your child is an infant prodigy and you feel that the world will not survive without his or her mathematical, linguistic or performing talents, you will have to take him to a special school which may well be situated at the other end of the city. Then your daily lot will be escorting the child there and back, or risking sending him alone by means of public transport. In rural districts, buses (or tractors, if the rains have turned the roads into running streams) may be provided to take a child from a distant village to school, but often he gets his first lesson in *terpenie* by having to walk several miles along a country road, a spectacular sport on an icy winter's day.

Three foreign languages – English (the favourite), German and French – are supposed to be available to Russian schoolchildren, but in most schools only one foreign language is taught, often inadequately. Russians are just beginning to understand that a foreign language is a must if you want a career. In Soviet times it was considered a useless extra, like drawing or singing, when compared with such important subjects as mathematics or chemistry. For why learn the language of an enemy unless you want to become a foreign spy? Besides, even if written foreign language was useful in some cases, the oral version was utterly superfluous: who were you going to talk to?

Some school subjects, like maths or chemistry, are studied

at considerably greater depth than by Western children of the same age. A good Russian secondary school student of mathematics could help a first-year European university student pass his exams.

Gold and silver school medal winners may enter university without having to sit entrance examinations. This is a major advantage as competition for places at institutions of higher learning is fierce. A good education has always been prestigious and generates respect. Girls with an education are a much more attractive goal for a choosy male. For their part, many boys would rather go to university than join the army, and conscription rules allow a postponement for university students. It's not that boys particularly like learning, but it's a softer option to wile away your time dozing in the back seat of the classroom than to spend it marching.

University examinations in most cases are oral. It is much easier to persuade the professor you have said all there is to say about a subject when there is no written proof to the contrary. In their turn, the professors prefer this as it takes less time and saves a lot of energy. If you have failed an examination you can try again and again. Officially you cannot go on indefinitely, but in reality with persistence you may drive the professor to despair, shuddering at the sight of you and signing anything to get you out of his sight.

Educators' salaries are in inverse proportion to the height of the education ladder. Often the monthly pay of a common labourer far exceeds that of a poor university professor. Fortunately, some would still rather be a professor than a labourer.

There are no university campuses in the Western sense. Universities seldom have buildings built specially for them. More often than not, they are assigned buildings scattered all over the city, and it is not uncommon for a student to travel from one end of the city to the other for a lecture or tutorial. Students either live at home, in rented rooms, or in madhouses, erroneously called hostels.

Many parents pull strings to get their offspring into university. Their success varies depending on how important the applicant happens to be, or how great the sum attached to the string.

Leisure and Pleasure

Getting Pickled

Every Russian knows that you are nobody without your *dacha*, a summer house with a little garden attached. There is no flower nonsense in the garden; give a Russian good tomato seedlings, and he'll show you what he can do. In the autumn there will be tens of kilos of first-rate tomatoes. He may not know what to do with them – his family won't look at tomatoes any more, and the nearest shop is already full of tomatoes – but they are his own creation, he has watered them all summer and watched them grow. Who cares if they work out three times more expensive than if he had bought them?

A Russian riddle asks: 'What bug has a brown back, a white front and feet all covered in manure?' The answer is: 'The dacha owner.' He is exhausted, he has had two heart attacks working in sweltering heat and in pouring rain, he roundly curses his plot (and his lot), but try and take it from him and he will fight like a bear disturbed in his den in the midst of winter.

There are good reasons for all this. The Russians always have to be on the alert, for they never know what the future has in store. Also, everybody knows that vodka is best when accompanied by a well-pickled cucumber, and it is only at home that the best pickles are made. A Russian who has not pickled at least a hundred kilos of cucumbers, green tomatoes and peppers, plus a barrel of cabbages, will be looked upon with pity and compassion: he must either be ill or too lazy. Or maybe he hopes that his grandmother who lives in the country will share her huge store. And she probably will – hardly anyone is ever able to eat all that they have preserved.

Winter Wonderland

The Russians love snow. It may cost the authorities a fortune to salt and clear the streets and to dislodge the icicles poised to drop like daggers from the cities' balconies and metal roofs, but winter is welcomed like an old friend. It is not just the sight of snow-clad streets and trees, the vast snowy fields, the frozen snow-covered rivers and lakes that is adored by all. People enjoy going about in the snow, and look forward to getting out their furs and heavy clothes which have been carefully stored in mothballs.

Those who can afford it go off to camps in the country where they stay in comfortable warm apartments and spend a few days skiing, sledging, skating, walking in the snowy forests, and going to the sauna. This is also an opportunity for them to enjoy *shashlyk* – meat roasted on a spit over an open fire outside. Russians like barbecues, even in winter.

A favourite pastime, exclusively male, is winter fishing. Fishing is popular in any season, but in winter when there is no sense in going to the dacha, men flock to nearby rivers, often right in the city centres, in the hope of catching fish. The frozen rivers are studded with thickly-clad figures, immovable over the holes they have made in the ice. With very short rods they lure the fish to bite. Most of the time their catch is the delight of their cat; besides, with the rivers that flow through cities being heavily polluted, even if the unlucky fish is bigger than your palm, eating it would be a sort of Russian roulette.

(If you go fishing in a small stream well away from the cities, however, things may be different, for Russian fish are no less hardy than Russians themselves, and a Russian perch will survive where his Western brethren would long since have breathed their last.)

Besides being a healthy habit, winter fishing has another attractive side. It is very chilly sitting on the ice for hours when the temperature is well below zero. The only way to prevent yourself from catching your death of cold is to take along a bottle of vodka. How can your wife possibly object to your using this universal medicine to stay alive?

Dreaming of a Lucky Break

Russians love to dream about sudden wealth. One of the most popular Russian fairy tales is about a lazybones called Emelya and a magic pike. Emelya spends his life lying on the warm stove in his peasant hut. One day he goes to the river to fetch water, but instead he draws out a big pike which possesses magical powers. The pike gives him the power to turn wishes into reality. "The Pike Commands and I Demand!" shouts Emelya, and without stirring a finger he gets his heart's desire from buckets of water which walk home by themselves, to marrying a princess, to conjuring up a table cloth which, on command, will set itself with all sorts of good things. The moral of the story is that your fate does not depend on your being good or bad, just lucky.

A favourite Russian word is 'khalyava', something you have got for nothing. It does not matter what it is – a free ticket to a show you would never care to attend otherwise, a badge or a booklet that a firm is handing out free and which you would never dream of reading, or an invitation to a restaurant from an interested businessman. The Russians firmly believe in not examining the teeth of a gift horse. A gift is a gift is a gift.

Lotteries of all kinds are popular in Russia. Millions of people are fooled by the so-called financial pyramids where you invest a few *roubles* and are promised a million the day after tomorrow. As pyramid after pyramid takes a tumble and the crooks are arrested and sentenced, new crowds of Russians enthusiastically line up for another sweet dream.

Family Forays

Visiting relatives is a favourite pastime. At the weekend, when Westerners will happily drive miles out of town to enjoy a barbecue on a beach, Russians (if it is not summer and there is no need to water the tomatoes) will go on family visits. The whole family, including great-grandmother and new-born babies, solemnly walks out to the bus stop loaded with home-made biscuits and pickles. Their relatives may live at the other end of the town, but it will probably make the outing more fun. Villagers may walk several miles to see relatives in another village (unless they have a car, of course). On arrival, they will drink vodka, discuss different recipes and watch South American soaps (what else is left to view, now that the they've stopped showing the Indian ones?).

Hooked on TV

Watching soaps has become a national craze. When a popular soap opera is on, the police may take a breather since all the criminals are off the streets sitting in front of the (stolen) TV, weeping over the sad fate of José and his Manuella, or Clara or Rosita. In the past if asked about some event a Russian might have said that it had occurred last year before Easter, or after Lent, or on All Saints' Day. Now he may tell you that it was somewhere between the

126th and 130th episode of *Santa Barbara*.

Russians no longer go the cinema – they don't have to. When you can sit at home in front of your television screen and watch the latest film, live or on video, from Hollywood or by your favourite Russian director, why should you bother going elsewhere to watch the same thing? The culture channel, with ballet programmes and classical concerts, is also popular, although Russians enjoy dressing up and going to live performances.

One programme Russians try not to miss is *The Field of Miracles*. Viewers shout encouragement at the screen as contestants try to guess a word, then another, then another. The whole country watches them, nervous and sweating over a word of four letters, beginning with a 'd' and ending with an 'n', which is not what you have just thought it was. They may (or may not) end up with a sum of money. Really big wins are, of course, rare.

Programmes are broadcast from Moscow across the nation's 11 time zones, which means that Muscovites see the six o'clock news when they sit down to dinner, whereas the citizens of Okhotsk, in far eastern Russia, wake up to the same programme with their breakfast.

What is Sold Where

Russian shops today differ from shops of ten years ago as much as the boudoir of Marie-Antoinette differed from a prison cell. The counters of food departments are crammed with all sorts of eatables. For instance, whereas until recently there was only 'no cheese' or 'cheese', and nobody would dream of asking what sort of cheese it was, now there are dozens of different kinds, both home produced and imported. In Soviet times, with luck, you might buy a whole chicken; now heaps of chicken legs are brought in from America (nicknamed Bush's legs, because their importation began in the days of President Bush senior). Not only is meat offered for sale, but you can have your choice, an amazing situation for a Soviet citizen.

Strange combinations of goods may be displayed in the same shop. Shoes and perfume, children's toys and medicine, video tapes and tin openers can lie side by side, as privatized establishments sublet their floor space to anyone who is willing to pay for it. But there is a spoonful of tar in this delicious barrel of honey. The prices in Russia are close to Western ones, but the salaries and wages are a tiny fraction of those in Western Europe.

At street corners dried sunflower seeds are sold in small glass measures by old women. Russians love sunflower seeds, especially when eaten in company and combined with healthy gossip. The peculiar characteristic of these seeds is that once you have begun them, you can't seem to stop until the last seed is cracked and eaten. Some people are very skilful at this and contribute substantially to the litter in the streets by spitting out the husks at Kalashnikov speed.

Custom and Tradition

Holy Days and Holidays

The Communists introduced Communist holidays and declared all others null and void except New Year which was supposed to replace the bourgeois Christmas. But the Russians are a cunning lot and outwitted the powers-that-be by turning official holidays into intimate and private celebrations.

International Women's Day (8 March), which marks women fighting for equal rights with men, was immediately interpreted as a sort of Mother's Day on which not only mothers but every female, from babies to elderly ladies of unidentifiable age, would be congratulated and offered gifts of all sorts, but most often flowers. Since there was no St Valentine's Day, young lovers usurped this holiday, and woe betide the young man who does not offer his girl at least a modest bunch of wild flowers. On this one day in the year, all Russian women are loved by all Russian men – a truly remarkable event.

The same thing happened with Army Day (23 February) which is the Russian equivalent of Father's Day. Every man will be congratulated whether he is a father or not, and this time it is young men who expect a small gift from their girlfriends. The Army doesn't mind, as the soldiers know that it's the day they have the right to drink double their normal amount.

New Year's Eve is utterly unlike the other holidays. To begin with, it is not quite clear what Russians celebrate. Before the Communist coup, the best festival of the year was Christmas. When the Communists crossed Christmas off the calendar, naturally the Christmas tree was off as well, both for religious and ecological reasons. But the sweet memories of the tree, the gifts, the warm atmosphere of the holiday were not to be annihilated so easily. In the course of time common sense prevailed, though in a somewhat distorted way. Christmas was definitely out, as God had been cancelled, once and for all.

But the Christmas tree came back victorious, disguised as a New Year tree. Everything was there, except, perhaps, the angels, replaced by Grandfather Frost and his granddaughter Snegurochka (the Snow Maiden). Everyone ignored the suspicious similarity between Grandfather Frost and St Nicholas (alias Santa Claus). The Bethlehem Star on the tree top was now the Communist five-pointed star. Thus the only major change was the shift of the date from 7 January (Christmas Day for Orthodox Christians) to the eve of 1 January. Any difficulty with this arrangement was easily overcome because you could always start the celebrations a week before the real date and go on till the real Christmas.*

New Year's Eve is without doubt the best holiday of the year, a genuine family celebration when people stay awake all night long, or at any rate the larger part of it, drinking, dancing and watching dull television shows of the lowest possible taste (unless they happen to be among the young people who prefer to see in the New Year in the midst of a forest, gathered around a living fir tree and a bonfire).

Next in importance is Victory Day, 9 May, marking victory over Germany in 1945. Outside Russia few remember that during the Second World War, though among those killed were some 357,000 British and 251,000 Americans, Russian losses approached 30 million. The day is celebrated by military parades, the biggest of which is in Moscow's Red Square.

Two major Soviet holidays are still observed – May Day (1 May), the day of International Solidarity of Working People, and the November Holiday (7-8 November), the date of the Bolshevik coup in Petrograd (St Petersburg) in 1917, proudly called The Great October Socialist Revolution. In Bolshevik times, both holidays were very grand affairs, with military demonstrations, general assemblies at absolutely every factory and school, however small, and joyful marches of the happy citizens of the country of victorious socialism through the streets of their cities and towns, often soaked to the skin or bent against a snowstorm, but still clinging to their posters and heavy portraits of the Communist leaders. If you wanted to stay away from this show of unanimous approval of Communist Party policy, you had to think up a very valid reason, or else.

* The Russians have two calendars – old style and new style – which gives them a unique opportunity to celebrate the same event twice, and they make ample use of it: two Christmases, two New Years, two Easters.

These days, on these two holidays only a handful of staunch Communist supporters march along the streets early in the morning, while the military sleep peacefully in their barracks. Both holidays have remained, for no-one, including fierce anti-Communists, is brave enough to cancel them altogether: the public would be furious. A holiday is a holiday, whatever the reason.

Now just seasonal holidays, the first is connected to spring and nature awakening, and the second to crop gathering, May Day being perfect for planting the potatoes, while 7 November is good for autumn house-cleaning. Both are celebrated with huge feasts, when food is consumed in gargantuan quantities and everyone goes home with their stomachs full, hiccuping happily. Foreigners invited to partake of a Russian festive table are normally carried away by a couple of riggers and are only able to think again about food several days later.

The post-Communist government, conscious of the necessity to provide not only bread but also circuses for the people, has made an attempt at setting up new holidays. One that has changed its name several times is celebrated on 12 June for two reasons: there are no other holidays in June, and it was on that day that the Russian Federation declared its independence not many years ago. Historians, politicians and journalists are still arguing who it was Russia got independence from.

Government

Efficiency Deficiency

There are said to be some countries in the world where the government is even less efficient than in Russia. Don't you believe it. There has never been an efficient adminis-tration in Russia from time immemorial. Efficiency and government in Russia are incompatible. This, at closer inspection, is not so very bad. When you know that you can expect little or nothing from your government, you feel free to act on your own.

Russians treat the law like a telegraph pole: you cannot jump over it, but you can go round it. The first thought a Russian has after a new law is introduced is how to circumvent or avoid it. It does not matter in the least what the law is about, because laws in principle cannot be good or useful to the man in the street. This is probably the only law every Russian would agree with. So, when you absolutely must not, but want to very much, you may.

More often than not a Russian will break the law even when he cannot gain much by doing so. He will cross the street at a red light or in the wrong place not because he is in a hurry but because it is such fun to break a rule.

The Western concept of liberty is not the same as that which the Russians call '*volya*'. *Volya* means that you are free to do what you like. Liberty is *volya* limited by law, a hateful idea for a Russian free thinker. The 19th-century conspirators who assassinated the Emperor Alexander II called their secret society *Narodnaya Volya*, The People's *Volya*. It was *volya* for the Russian people that they were dreaming about, not liberty or freedom.

Party Time

The Russian constitution says that Russia is a democracy, and you just have to believe this.

The parliament has two chambers. The lower chamber is called the Duma, from the Russian word *dumatj*, to think. If nothing else, the name is meant to create the impression that some thinking is done there, though in reality nothing could be further from the truth. The upper chamber, called The Federation Council, is made up of representatives of the regions, well paid functionaries who are supposed to lobby the interests of their territories.

Under the Communists there was only one party, the Communist Party of the Soviet Union (CSPU), often referred to simply as The Party. At election time there was only one candidate for each post – either a Party member or a non-Party member, the latter carefully selected by the Communists. Thus the so-called 'block of Communists and non-Party members' always emerged victorious.

Today there are scores of parties, from Communists to anarchists to extremists to nihilists and the Beer Fans Party, and all are eager to recruit as many new members as possible. But the memory of the Communist Party with its iron fist and the unsmiling face of a KGB functionary is still fresh. "No, sir, thank you very much for your interest in me, but I don't feel ready for membership of anything yet."

Sharing Not Stealing

The Russians are discussing the possibility of raising the salaries of the leading political figures tenfold or more in the hope that they will steal less. This is a good idea which has only one small disadvantage: a corrupt official will steal irrespective of how much he earns officially; he cannot stop even if he wants to because he has to work closely with his friends and is bound by certain obligations.

Officials stole in the days of Ivan the Terrible, they stole in the days of Peter the Great, they stole under Stalin, and there is every chance that they will follow the same pattern for ever and ever. It's part of the job, in a way. You cannot sit on a barrel of honey and not try a spoonful.

Business

Russians hate business. All businessmen are crooks by definition. As a Russian proverb says, 'Honest work won't get you a stone palace'. If an American meets a millionaire, his first thought is, "What a clever man he must be!" The first thought of a Russian is sure to be, "How has this crook managed to grab so much?"

A popular joke goes:

"What is the Russian way to do business?"
"To steal a crate of vodka, sell it, then spend the proceeds on buying drink."

Not many Russians make trading their occupation. Everybody agrees that it is utterly immoral to buy cheap and sell at a higher price. Merchants and shop-owners are well known for their greed: "Blood-suckers of the poor proletariat, that's what they are. The Bolsheviks were right to have shot them, the rascals." With such a philosophy, running a business in Russia is for the audacious, not to say brave.

Winston Churchill is rumoured to have exclaimed once in exasperation, 'For those Russians, to lose an hour is to lose nothing!' A good example of Russian time-keeping would be the 'five-minute conferences' before the beginning of each working day at Russian factories; these may last for an hour or more.

Russians are quick learners. The fall of Communist ideology has brought about an understanding that first come is first served. The Russian bear in his den has stirred visibly. Hibernation time is over. New companies are emerging and new business relations developing. Outdated laws are being replaced by sounder ones. Still, a good kick from behind would help to speed up matters no end.

Culture

Ask a Russian to name part of his face and he will say "Nose". Ask him to name a domestic bird and it will be "Chicken" for certain. And if you ask him to name a poet, his response will be "Pushkin". To say that Russians adore Pushkin is to state the obvious. They gloat over the name, they swear by it; when someone does not do what he ought to, his friend is sure to ask sarcastically, "OK, who will do that for you, then? Pushkin?"

The Russians have much to boast about culturally. As well as great writers and playwrights such as Tolstoy, Chekhov and Dostoyevsky, world-famous Russian names include composers like Tchaikovsky, the world's best chess players, the Bolshoi and Kirov ballets, and *Hamlet* which Russians claim is a Russian play. Hardly a drama theatre does not stage *Hamlet* once in a while because its hero is the very image of that unique Russian class, the intelligentsia. Like all intellectuals, he is fond of walking to and fro, asking the audience whether he should or should not be.

All through Russian history Russian authors have had to learn how to say something critical without risking a prison sentence or death. The period of learning was hard, with many of them proving poor pupils. But those who stayed alive were skilful at speaking metaphorically, and everybody understood that what was said was not at all what was meant. Before Gorbachev, the following saying was popular: "Don't think it; if you have thought it, don't say it; if you have said it, don't write it down; if you have written it down, don't publish it; if you have published it, immediately say you're sorry." With the advent of *glasnost* (openness), you are free to express the wildest idea possible. But what?

According to a popular poet, in Russia a poet is more than just a poet. The creative artists' fight for survival served as a stimulant, a catalyst to creativity. Anyone can produce entertaining literature; but to offer the world a masterpiece, you have to have suffered. Authors and musicians, painters and sculptors are painfully looking for new ways to express themselves. Not many succeed. As one wit had it, "The only future that great Russian literature seems to have is its glorious past."

Although Russian nationalists might not agree, during the last few centuries Russian artists developed under strong French, and later English and American, influence. As a result a very original art form has emerged, something Russians are justly proud of, although Russian painters have not distinguished themselves sufficiently to be noticed by the West.

Icon painting is an art form with which there is nothing to compare. The greatest icon painter, Andrej Roublev, worked in the 14th and 15th centuries, was forgotten by his compatriots, and was only brought back from oblivion at the end of the 19th century. Russian icon painters did not attempt to copy nature; they tried to paint an ideal, something that cannot be seen with the naked eye. The icon is not an image of a living person, it is his soul, the very essence of the man.

Book Lovers for Life

Russians take special pride in books for children. "You must write for children like you write for adults, only better." And they do. Among illustrious children's authors are Marshak, Tchukovski and Zakhoder. Zakhoder has written a Russian version of *Alice in Wonderland* which has become a children's favourite. Among foreign authors, the young enjoy Hans Andersen, the Brothers Grimm and Charles Perrault. They also love *Pippi Longstocking, Mary Poppins, Winnie-the-Pooh* and *Carlson Who Lives on the Roof.* Young Russian book lovers may be envied by all.

Adults read mostly in buses and trains, which has helped Russins to win the reputation of the most avid readers in the world. Since they spend half their time on public transport or at bus stops waiting for a bus, it's no wonder they are considered the best-read people ever.

Crime and Punishment

The notion of crime is somewhat blurred in Russia. For what, after all, is a crime? If you are a factory worker and before going home you pocket a few items you have made with your own hands, surely it is not a crime. There is special terminology for this: people do not steal, they 'carry spare parts out', which is a quite different thing. And what secretary will buy paper for her own use when there is such a lot in her boss's filing cabinet? And it pays off, you know. A bird pecks a seed at a time. Today you bring home one wheel, tomorrow another, and in a little while there's a car.

In Soviet times there was more punishment than there was crime; now crime has taken an impressive lead. In the days of Stalinist rule, you might meet in prison very respectable professors, world-famous scientists, philosophers, philologists and army generals. It was not much fun to find yourself stuck for life in such company in a small cell with barred windows and a concrete floor, but these days your fellow inmates might well be murderers and burglars, many of them ill with TB. It would be pointless trying to pass the time discussing existentialism with them.

Russia is still behind the United States in crime rate statistics, but is making good progress and given a chance will soon catch up. Most crime is connected with encroachment on other people's property which is not surprising: when someone is poor, his first thought is to make the richer man share, by force if necessary. If Bolsheviks did that with the whole country, why shouldn't you imitate them on a smaller scale?

The days when you might leave your house without locking your door are gone, and gone for ever. The most eloquent sign of the changing times is metal latticed ground-floor windows in every city. Some of the lattices are quite attractive, but this is not their chief aim.

Other kinds of crime are not far behind. Alcohol abuse has acquired a good companion, use of drugs – not as much as in Amsterdam, but the Russians do their bit.

As for juvenile delinquency, well, youngsters do not carry guns to school nor shoot their classmates and teachers. Not yet. But there's always room for development.

Russian police are called militia and are the object of endless jokes and derision, especially by criminals and frustrated drivers. People are beginning to realize that the police may sometimes be of use, though the police themselves make every effort to dissuade them. The most noticeable section of the police is the OMON, an abbreviation for the special detachment sent whenever and wherever something out-of-the-ordinary happens, such as a scuffle between football fans or a minor war on Russian territory.

Every year thousands upon thousands of Russians are stopped by police for drunk driving. Road accidents and casualties are multiplying, and the harsher the punishment, the more defiant the drivers become. Every Russian is fond of driving fast, and fast driving is so much more fun when you're tipsy. The chief reason why the traffic police are so hated is that they don't appreciate this.

When a policeman stops you for exceeding the speed limit, he may ask if you'd like to pay a small fine or a big fine. Always answer that the fine should be small, and don't ask for a receipt. Policemen have wives and families, like everyone else.

Ruthless Rogues

Thugs of the Al Capone type have always been present on the Russian stage. But with the swift change of political regime, they have multiplied and become very noticeable. No longer awkward about openly demonstrating their wealth and influence, they adorn themselves with heavy gold chains and their clothes are characterised by their utter lack of taste.

Many of them make money by racketeering, with the owners of even the smallest kiosks having to pay for protection. About half the national income is said to be controlled by illegal enterprises. Even large institutions often prefer to pay up rather than face unpleasantness – from blackmail to assassination – from the mafia. In such circumstances, naturally, the dividing line between legal and illegal transactions becomes blurred, and every manager and every director will admit that breaking a law or two on a daily basis is part of his job. Small wonder blackmail is rife: there's plenty for blackmailers to make use of.

There is every reason to believe that if a villa is bought by a Russian somewhere on the Mediterranean coast, it will belong to one of the three types: a superstar, a political figure, or a thug. Too often the distinction between the three is minimal.

Conversation

A favourite subject of conversation is politics. Every Russian, sane or otherwise, will tell you how bad things are politically, and what he would do if he were President. There isn't anyone who doesn't have an original plan for saving Russia from incompetent rulers, or a detailed plan for its economic development. The common feature of all these plans is an ardent desire to hang the present administration from the lampposts.

Unlike the English, Russians do not have the skill of talking about the weather all the way through a transatlantic cruise and back. They will hold forth about a great many things – politics, domestic affairs, the health of the younger daughter of their second cousin, or the concept of the Holy Trinity. However, there are a few subjects which Russians will tend to avoid and on which it is next to impossible to try to draw them out. They are very shy about sex matters, even in the doctor's consulting room, not to mention in front of friends or children or their parents. But with the advent of pornography and even (Oh, God!) sex shops, the attitude is becoming more relaxed. From every newspaper stand very modestly clad girls stare at you with promise in their eyes. One may now hear such formerly unmentionable words as condom, coitus, or group sex. Homosexual relations are still considered disgusting and repulsive, but are no longer punishable. Sex education is a complete taboo. Russians and, above all, educators still believe that parents find their babies in the cabbage patch, or buy them in elite shops for foreign currency.

Most Russian swear words are based on sex. Russians are proud that their curses are well known to sailors of every nation who rarely know what they are saying; if they did, they might think twice before employing such blood-curdling imprecations. Fortunately, Russians themselves seldom think about what they are saying.

Among the most used swear words are *mat* (pronounced 'mut'), where the speaker insults his opponent by slandering his mother, as well as *blyadj* (whore) and *sukin syn* (son of a bitch). A recent addition to the list of swear words and deemed insulting enough to start a fight is *kozyol* (billy-goat).

Language

Every Russian would agree that the Russian language has all the good characteristics of other languages and none of their deficiencies. It is as melodious as Italian, as domineering as German, and as precise as English.

One of its best qualities is the possibility of expressing minute nuances of meaning with the help of an infinite number of suffixes. For example, *Loshadj* is just a horse, while *loshadka* is a gay little adorable thing, and *loshady-onka* is an exhausted working horse, well on in years and bent under its load. If you want to use an endearment you may call it your *loshadushka*, but if you mean a big and clumsy animal, it will be *loshara,* and so on.

There is little an English lover can do with the name of his belovéd Mary, but his Russian rival can use any one of a host of pet names for the same girl, such as Marya, Marijka, Marisha, Marja, Mara, Marulya, Mulya, Marusya, Musya, Masya, Masyata, Maryuta, Maryukha, Maryusha, Musha, Manya, Manyunja, Manyura, Manyusha, Manyatka, Maka, Masha, Mashanya, Mashonya, Mashuka, Mashunya, Munya, Mashura, Mura, Shura, Mashara, Muta, Mashukha, Morya, Maryushka, Maryasha, all of them terms of endearment. (If he is angry with her, he may add to her name the derogatory suffix 'k', as in Mashka, Man'ka, Nyus'ka, etc.) Clearly, the Russian suitor stands a much better chance of winning a girl's heart than his West European or American rival. Nor does he ever get confused as to who is who in Russian novels.

Russian has a few drawbacks. It is said that English is an easy language to learn to speak badly, and one of the most difficult to learn to speak well. Russian is difficult in both ways. Nobody, including the Russians themselves, speaks it correctly. Writing it is a worse nightmare, best demonstrated each year at the university entrance exams.

In Russian there are more 'buts' than rules, and every 'but' has to be learnt by heart by the unfortunate victims of the learning process. For instance the word '*zhare(n)ny*' (fried, roast) should be spelled with one 'n' if it is an adjective as in *zhareny gus* (roast goose), but with two 'n's if it is a passive participle and is accompanied by some descriptive adverb; in that case some prefix is also necessary: *khorosho zazharenny gus* (well-fried goose). Another stumbling block is punctuation. There is no logic whatever. It just has to be remembered that before a subordinate clause one should place a comma. Pause, or no pause, don't forget the comma. Why? What's it there for? Don't be silly, because it's always been there.

Such an attitude is very characteristic of the Russian way of thinking. Some years ago the Academy of Sciences proposed a modest spelling reform, cancelling the most atrocious exceptions to the rules. It met with public outcry. Labourers and lecturers, army men and men of letters, ministers and members of parliament, all rose up in arms against the reform. The chief reason was that if they spent years learning to spell, why should anybody else escape the ordeal?

A number of Russian words like balalaika, bolshevik, collective farm, intelligentsia, dacha, steppe, tundra, vodka are used by English speakers. One word, 'sputnik' (the first Russian earth satellite), became so famous that the suffix '-nik' was added to form new English words, like 'refusnik'.

However, the English language has had rather more influence on Russian. Before the Second World War, most borrowed words were German; during and after the war, they were English, and English only. Some of the borrowed words are quite specific. A stylish youngster may proudly declare, "I've bought new 'shoosy'", by which he means shoes, but you are mistaken if you think that the word is distorted because his English is close to pidgin. The ruthlessly disfigured word means exclusive footwear, most certainly imported. For cheap Russian merchandise he will scornfully use the Russian word.

The Author

Born in Leningrad, as St Petersburg was called in Communist times, Vladimir Ilyich Zhelvis managed to survive the terror of Stalin's purges as well as the carnage of the Second World War (he was in Leningrad during the German siege and famine). After all that it was quite easy to live through the times of post-war havoc, when he made ample use of the general confusion and got a university education. He then went to the Far East, where he met his future wife with whom he had two daughters.

Family life did not prevent him from writing two dissertations, philological and psycholinguistic, and a book on the psychological and social aspects of swearing. He can swear in approximately 80 languages, which helps him a lot in his teaching career, as he now lives in the ancient Russian city of Yaroslavl with Stella, his wife, and his Doberman, Cliff, and lectures to students at the local Pedagogical University.
